A COLOMBER IN THE ⸻

also by Lyndon Davies

HYPHASIS (Parthian 2006)

SHIELD (Parthian 2010)

A COLOMBER IN THE HOUSE OF POESY

Lyndon Davies

AQUIFER

Published in the United Kingdom in May 2014 by

Aquifer Books,
Glasfryn,
Llangattock,
Powys
NP8 1PH
www.glasfrynproject.org.uk

ISBN: 978-0-9928438-0-9

Cover image by Penny Hallas

Acknowledgements.
Some of these poems originally appeared in Poetry Wales, Fire,
LPBmicro, Scintilla, Roundyhouse.

Heartfelt thanks to Scott Thurston and David Greenslade.

CONTENTS

A COLOMBER IN THE HOUSE OF POESY

ESTUARINE

ODDMENTS

A COLOMBER IN THE HOUSE OF POESY

Scaletones

"It is a tremendous, mysterious shark, more clever than man. For reasons that perhaps no one will ever know, it chooses its victim, and when it has chosen, it pursues him for years and years, for his entire life, until it has succeeded in devouring him."

> Dino Buzzati - *(Il Colombre, 1966.* Translated as *The Colomber)*

"Ah indeed I cast my net into their sea and hoped to catch fine fish; but I always drew out an old god's head."

> Friedrich Nietzche - *Thus Spoke Zarathustra* ('Of Poets')

"What suddenly comes to light in Emily Bronte's attitude, by means of an intangible moral solidity, is the dream of a sacred violence which no settlement with organised society can attenuate."

> Georges Bataille - *Literature and Evil*

"Il est, hélas! des coureurs sans répit"

> Charles Baudelaire - 'Le Voyage' from *Les Fleurs du Mal*

Emil: O, who has done this deed?
Des: Nobody, I myself, farewell:

> William Shakespeare - *Othello* (Act V Sc ii)

The Patient One

The colomber, humbler
than most mythical animals,
waits in the offing,
makes no demands,

yearns only, or not *yearns*
but has its nature,
that one delivery to make
in the House of Poesy.

God help the colomber
in the House of Poesy.

A Romance

Issue arising (this sad art):
to wit, no anthem for exiles.
Dust
negating justice.
           Gist:
every egg a
bird, every flop a corpse.

                   There's this sodden
paddling of hands -
a version. The moustache
of Vlad percolates the briny
nog of Emily.

Seduction Theory

No, it's three pm Friday February the twenty second,
hour of the dupe, anno domini two thousand and eleven...
Treachery drips from the leaves and doves scatter,
pumping, white tracks of the ever-rolling gouts
keep fraying-off into the furrows
of a man's brow, boot polish spattering the flags -
who would have believed it? (Time to settle your accounts
and get out). Some kind of awakening, then, can we call it that?
Or fissure? (A shudder of prosthetic buttock).
We're talking here of an incomparable spinner of fabulations
snagged in a rig of someone else's making:
he never quite believed sufficiently in the ones he'd blagged,
that's obvious, though she believed in them, she pinned them
high on her wall, was in this his amanuensis
and creator. For which she must be as good as gold
at all times, as true as muck, his princess, or he would give her
                                          what she deserved,
by sword, by hand, by silk, whether in a public space
or privacy of the chamber where she resembles heaven.

Property

Bring on the very chaise-longue
where they gasped their lives away,
each one of them in her turn.
                              A midden's
lascivious fume violating the hill's
sweet heather.

Everything but the night
ran off in a panic, scarpered. You needn't
worry about it,
it's not your
ossuary.

Offering

We put milk out in a silver chalice
food for the ones who run continually
and can never stop running and staring
into that chalice where the milk's gone,

as if there was always one arriving there before them,
no wonder they're hungry and afraid,
continually on the qui vive,
running and running, which can be very tiring.

There's never anything left in that vessel but a pearl,
like a bead of milk. They run all day
continually from whatever it is that is coming after them
and going before them, guzzling what they crave,

leaving just a pearl. It's already too late, though, for the pearl,
too late to stop running, it always was too late
to give up believing in the monster
who drank the milk. But did the sparrows drink it?

Promissory
For Kevin Mills

Matter is subtle here if surprisingly projective.
At every turn of the stair some old wag
waits with a hailer cocked: genuinely grand
television-style personality. My house
is not my house,
down there in the fizz, in the atom-bed: freaks, pangs,
erotomania of extravagantly exclusive nightwear,
though enzymes have already eaten away half
time's stuff,
at the base, as opposed to the hyperstructure
poised for decorum's sake. One muse one vote,
no apple no cry, that's the rule in the jury-box;
if a bowl pings you know it's honest ,
but you still have to go through the process,
honour your promissory note. Is this pleasure or work?
Dread waits in the road, its big open mouth slobbering like a cave.
My book is not my book.

Leaves

Their voices are happy
already now in the leaves
are happy are happy
as leaves are when a wind shakes them

when a wind scatters them
are happy because
a wind scatters them and they fall
where the wind takes them

according to the law
according to the promise made
by a metaphorical angel
are happy because

a wind coming from afar
has taken them and they fall
where they must fall
and can fall

according to a promise made
by a metaphorical angel
mourned by the wind
verified by the wind's sadness and fury

are happy because
of the wind's swiftness and the wind's bounty
resembling heaven
its voices their own voices

are happy because
of their own swiftness and their own bounty
falling where they must
and can

The Dream of the Builder

Let's face it: he couldn't even build a wall
to bunker our dustbin, forgetting to overlap
the bricks, if ever he knew (which I doubt);
and here I am asking him to build a house
for the lost, since they must have a house - the trends
are worrying, not just there, and I thought
she'd miss it, that fellowship of the seamless, the flowing,
the knowing; especially the gentler who weren't
ever bad, (they can stay when they like, not the others though).

A house is a nest of vacancies held together
by trim. I chose him, I thought he could wing it,
trample its shape in the bracken. Whatever,
it wouldn't stand long or pretty and that would suit us.

But no he said no, he wasn't coming to build anything,
he'd just come to show her the way.
Find someone else.

Psychopomp

It's the insouciance which makes it shocking
and remote. There they are, ducking round and back
on the wind's shoulder. You think, so it's normal
(isn't it?): she's left the gas on, he's forgotten his coat,
his cash, his ribbons for the staff... High up there
the moon's just a withered calyx; down here,
every step's a caution. Perhaps, though, in the end,
his turning honours her natural disposition -
by which I don't mean indifference, I mean maternal poise.
But who cares? We've a hell of a way to travel
before we touch and mend, with hysterical
ellipses and landscapes difficult to get your head round,
in fact only barely sniffed at... Now suddenly
it's over? All over as far as he's concerned
apparently, without consulting me. How tall
he was, like a man on a podium, though bent
just now, like a man reaching over to open a shed door.

Research

Look out, a colomber is watching through binoculars,
a colomber is always locking on.
It's a stalker, a peeping tom.
Beware, beware.

You have to think of it as a free-standing nightmare,
you have to think of it as a person singular
circumambulating a thornbush or moving in
on the little hanky snagged on a twig,
that little hanky sodden with love-juice.

Children's Hour

Who smirched the page?
Sweep, naughty Sweep.

Who scrubbed it clean?
Sooty. Good Sooty

a judgment is coming.
Go out and meet it.

Squeak.

Eurydice

The eyes deny it
they're not saying
or going
                    anywhere
her neophyte's
slow glide

measured
                    downward
                                        levelling
into a column-grove

leaf-glints
and dew

all offered innocence
all offered
time

refusing even refusal's
incipient pause
at the gate
            voluptuary
tracking-back

tracking-back
her gaze

remains
her gaze
is having none of it

Hanged Man

He shows everyone
the way to the apple-stash
we follow this gash
up the street wondering

imagine walking though
from a room having lain
awake all night
or having woken early

tying that knot
highly specialized extravaganza
skill the absurd lurch
into nowhere

or just leaning down calmly
into a blotched grimace
tag in the air
secured threading the hyperstructure

don't do it we will regret it
according to parameters
a sleep a fruit
weep my lute

he carried through
Vlad hangs on his knees loving him in his way
all tongue was he happy
to taste the coffee

this cup (mine) smells of earth
or chick-peas the last drink
rarely lives up to its billing
I would like to grieve more

but knew him little
praise him without whorls
or particular decorum
who turned away

from it all owing something
nothing a note flipped
from his hand as he knotted
the threads dropped

even this being literature
picked over held up
assailed in a jury box
each whisper turned septic

he has the view now
over everything that was keeping him
consolations dandled
between the covers

health in the sick-bed
shelter for the pursued
enlightenment for the cozened
lithium for the overexcited

he is who we want him to be
a full stop
like a dot of pond mud
swarming with animalculae

Gothic

You'd swear she was only waiting for that moon, sly puck,
to pluck, to throw off her winding-sheet - devil take
the maid - having learned how to chasten her afflictions
to the civilities of the house. Climbing up
that night amazed out of the book,
she'd become a prize, he'd carry her image through the stations
far out into the mistlands of wherever on earth it is
he goes. No-one there would recognize her,
know her as he did. Assuming she was going to fall
very far, to very little purpose, he'd impale her
as iconic. No-one would believe she sighed
for the wound's sake because they wanted her to sigh
for his sake, or stay there finally when a bell croaked
on the inferior solemnity of a brideless evening,
hearing the stamp of heels, a piano and a hurdy-gurdy
from the living room hung with black drapes.

The Art of Oratory
1.

He said,
this is where you speak from, punching
himself in the gut, this snake-pit, low down here
in the burial-chamber. Let your words buzz
on your lips. You're getting there when the words buzz
on your lips, he said, tipping the bottle. Fuck,
he said. We call that triple resonance.
That's how you speak when you want to make someone listen.

Man of Sorrows

Everything slopes, recoils, keels away
from The Me. This is how it is and will be:
getting your face kicked-in by a cold shoulder,
your wink defiled by a snook regular
as clockwork. It's no use trying to revive
the mystery of the consummation in a mirror -
featuring who? Not anyone you can blame,
ahead of you and chasing the game through a door marked
Bliss: scribbled on, burnt in with a branding iron,
scored with a sword... The prophets are all cock:
you know what they're going to mean before they tell it,
you know what it's going to cost before they sell it,
because of the past which is not now.
But then he turns, or she turns, and everything opens up.
Imagine the innocence of a nape.

Shade

She thought I'd come out
to speak with her, she thought
I had called her. I hadn't,
I was merely muttering and trying
to walk where she'd walked.

Apprentice
1. *Vietnam*

All the stars in heaven,
like a radiant ambush,
burst on my head.
I was spinning, wobbling
out of control, shocked
to be taken seriously
by light, and anyway
utterly washed-up,
like the street I fell in.
Wherever I pitched or yawed,
defeat in the flower-beds,
lamias spitting gall
in trite rooms. By dragging
my threads through the dust
I made the rooks cackle.
Girls ran away from me.

I became delirious.
Before I had begun
distinguishing the chords
and putting them all together
in the shape of an offering,
behold - a sign,
a great flail thrashing low
over Younghusband's wood,
and over the church to the biscuit factory,
like a travelling ambush:
whirligigs, domes, spikes
of fire. The roofs bled.
It was all I could do
to stay, all I could do.

Hunted

Breaking bushes, set off diagonally.
Is it war - the sleeper in the palimpsest

of given window deploying birdseed,
chewy objects for puppy-love? Neglect

settles in forever over the city.
Think of a number, multiply by one,

move on. No tail on the omnibus or decision
regarding lingerie. Leave by a back exit

through trivial lanes, patched alleyways to the river.
Gratifying to bleed alone on a bridge:

one nibbled wrenched face mooning a parapet.
Wants to reap what he owed in the afternoon,

delete what he sowed. He can hear it sighing
but cannot recover impetus. Move on,

in all probability circling the chalice.
Good to believe in that covenant,

moving in.

Apprentice
2. Rollscourt Avenue

It was just one thing after another,
one debt, one dead-end after another
dead-end; one riff, one fallacy after another.

Fear in the cracks,
in the warp and weft; shit
hanging about, old muesli, grease in the gas-flues;
fruit-flies, silverfish, mould,
dry-rot.
One step after another,
one massacre after another.

Round and round the table,
round and round the chair,
round and round the mirror,
round and round the fire.

The table distant,
the chair warped,
the fire witless,
the mirror empty.

Grit in the sheets, verdigris in the saxophone-bell.

In Camera

Vlad craps in his bowler hat,
as Mangeclous had Vronsky
cross-eyed, jittering for release
after his melon feast, locking the door
on Anna to 'write the sonnet'
of their new-fledged love, fumbling as he squats
a nocturne on the pianoforte
to gild the din. Does Emily on a higher floor
gratefully bend to her task, tutu
puffed: a god-given opportunity,
letting a few great and small
blessedly out into the gaslight
par dessus le texte, her gut wrenched
with the wonder of it all,
agonized retention
bound by sublimities?

When the dupe returns,
knocking down all the walls in the house,
the place smells like a cross
between a midden and a brothel,
perfume scattered everywhere
and the bowler hidden in a bookcase.

None of this can be spoken of.
None of this none of this can be spoken of.

Word

They fear the word:
it comes from the secret
places; it reeks
of the intimacies, blazons
night's order of magnitude,
spits in the face
of a white hanky.

They love the word,
it's not theirs, they possess it
every time anew
like Christmas, they squander it
like an undeserved inheritance.
Many cling
at the hem sucking there.

History

And then out over the roofs out and on out
over the roofs and on out over
the roofs and so on: this is how we scrabble,
dare (an importunate matter of solidarity),
although one needn't. Gathering in the cracks -
a crumb here, a grain and a crumb
there; aquilegias and hollyhocks
bustling up through the rubble. We didn't need
to think of it as rubble, it was already fruit
in our fists, that rubble of the forms, smelling
of mothers and children, fathers and children,
kindly as earth smells of the showers
weltering down through wrack. I didn't seek
a flaw, there's no such thing, there are only
the sisters and brothers, the cousins and the neighbours,
stubborn as amaranths. Then the roofs,
of course the roofs, the roofs yes, and some big clouds
waving their squidgy arms. Squish squish
of the elements going in and out
of those clouds, and lava and foam. Peculiar
arousal of each innocent but delusional boot-heel.
God, that we tread, and me with a mandrill,
daring to wield it, too. I didn't need
a mandrill, I was only thinking of the sons
and daughters, oh the blank, the terrible, lying down alone.
Then somebody wept, then somebody threw a stone
from the absolute (involute) margin: they know
a thief when they see one - Look, he has come
for our trinkets. Snaffle him, roll him up

in the subtle but inert sympathies he brought with him
like a pox-filled blanket. Riddle him
deep with the sickness. He is a ghost
to all the others although himself not a ghost.

Sickbed

As time fades in the room
he considers the lily

gape of her lost stare.
She concedes her measure,

snogging her truth-map, spew
of degraded corpuscles.

Screw scuttering grooves
through bad air, all the fetid

waves running back, madcap
stir under a chaise-longue.

Cough cough she croaks
cough cough, it's tragic

for everyone, not for her.
Vlad settles a cushion,

he knows he will leave
quite soon on some elegant adventure.

Not yet, though, there's a sword
of virtue in this waiting,

blade with his name on, lamella
for probing the crack

of light under the earth's door,
hero, killer or both

or neither. What can he know
of a lustre beyond telling,

a gem tongued in a furrow
between one shore and another shore?

Commission

Perla,
perla della terra, pearl,
of no-one's world,
even this a question
built of saliva.

Must he now trail
or she to the four corners ailing
and adrift forever,
this intolerable treasure?

Perla,
perla della terra.

Seed

Emily loves the voices,
so many, so many
coming from far back,
scratchy and miniscule,

like a rug of cockroaches,
or mice in the conduits.
She feels responsible for them
but her heart's not in it

somehow since she arrived
in that chamber of singularities,
her heart a seed
of unimaginable genus.

She is quite prepared though
to carry its fruit back if they ask
one day if there is fruit.
They don't ask.

Lawn

Just because there's no obvious sign of damage
doesn't mean it's over, or mean
that nobody chanced their luck. In the end
that lawn's the proof, more clearly and more concisely
than a hand on a misericorde, or the soiled groan
of a solemn victim, parcelled-up, conveniently
muzzled there: all of which is theatre,
which is to say avoidance in the purest sense,
a matter of illumination and control,
although terrible in its rhetoric - we desired
one another's entrails, nothing less would do
(you see it in Bosch, in *The Crowning with Thorns*:
it's tenderness, no doubt, though tenderness for the wrong thing,
and avid and out of bounds). That lawn, though,
is the key, the necessary grace where the oaths are broken,
or lie down. And fade. Or don't fade. Now but not now.

Tribunal

All the just ones gathered sifting
sense, counter-sense:
no wonder a girl sweats
so, warps, puts herself
at a loss. Very old wags
blind in the mouth, scan
without insight or compassion,
close on a whisper
as pressure builds up rapidly,
importunate but remote,
passions shaped in the offing,
a vote, a note passing
from hand to hand,
though one arm paddling the fug's
enough for a gist
to pass muster or go down
trembling into the territories of extinction.

Did she swear
on love's book, tipping her bulb
of milk in a furrow,
honey dripped from a spoon?
She laps clods,
belonging in that place,
cynosure of evil willing,
charm of the lost,
the jealous, the wrong-skinned,
phthisic, apt in her nightwear;
hawks flubbering in a monogrammed
fazzoletto
as the plot sickens.

Reckoning

He follows her because he's lost and because it's written,
to the blackest room in the whitest tower,
because it's told, was whispered in what was given,
laid down, to the clearest deed in the blindest hour,

tweezer-gripping a hanky, that clunched give-away
addled with spunk, with blood, but is it bronchial
or chthonic? Blood anyway,
red for the shock, red for the energies of culmination.

It's not even a problem, it's just a fact
delivering him to his untimely act,
though not a bit silly
in his exotic garments, cloth of this and that, partly rent.

No occasion for doubt - princess run away quick
and be shriven elsewhere
in the white of the wake, run away, take your limbs
out there into the open, where no given or written is.

Listening

(For Susan Adams)

what

a tree listens
a wall listens

must

a field listens
a flame listens

I

a path listens
a cave listens
a crag listens
a picture-frame listens

do

a sky listens
a stone listens

say something say something

Madrigal

Was it there in Orlando Gibbons'
quietly cleaving bass-line ('Ah, Dear Heart'),
from A to B Flat overstepping the octave?

Or somebody else's constellated trouble,
tutti of howls? A trace,
that's to say
a sign which isn't a sign, a place
which is and isn't,

but may be a path elsewhere,
beyond the measure, the redoubt, but never
into the old principle, though never
with enough vehemence to go around:

the diminishing glint
of a departure once complete and withering.
I track its blip like the quivering
last tic of an earthquake,

over the porch of the ribs to the solar-plexus -
down to the feet already
fumbling a way of sorts
over banished pebbles.

Sea Level

Ice founders notional
emergency crack outsourced
through tide out of time's
layer-cake soot and organza
surge reverberation
unlocks adhesion-stacks
rearing and nodding like sea-fauns
as boards twist
first then disappear
under wallows she works quick
and gets over it before air
runs out jolly couch
rum complement of survivals
samplers and billet-doux
on the wave alive o
still waving o and alive o
as a prayer as a book
swung up like a grappling hook
light hurts where it sticks
no affinity for rescue
neither here nor wherever
the fever pays out
gross hectic as nigh plash tickles
cough in a drowned room
in a drowned house

Deposition

Up here it is motley
the light blows through it
making it ripple ah
the pleasures all to hand

never having to vex anyone
for the sake of a gist
and the chase over
the bowl shattered

lightness of floating here
but the others are coming
gathering drawing down
preparing the rituals

forms in their meetness
even this being literature
a question of comprehension
rewinds re-screenings

neither baffled nor fixed
but bristling all over with escape routes
I flew the leaves flew
in the wind happy

Gaze

Her gaze
remains. Her gaze
is having none of it.

Her looking on
his looking on
her looking on.

The Art of Oratory
2.

Speaking, don't think of speaking though, he said
he said, tipping a bottle, fuck
he said, until the whirligig of the unspoken
grieves at your tongue, and your tongue squeaks and falls off
and you see it waving at you from a distant pinnacle,
no longer approachable, but don't worry
it never really did belong to you
and the point is to grow another when the time comes, if it does,
although this will be difficult and at first impossible
which is what speaking is
when there are already too many pingbacks and no-one
is listening, not even me, I said listening
except the ones who have forgotten how to
he said tipping the bottle, fuck
he said

Cyprus

The Moor awaits his love
who's going away
to a coal-black country.

So beautiful, so depraved,
his dear.
'Ancor un bacio,' 'ancor...'

shimmering down from the tower.
It's happening,
it's here

(it's Friday, February the twenty seventh
and so on).
The Moor awaits his crime.

A colomber gravitates,
veers laterally.

O vision where's thy sting?
Ethereal neat doves swoop,
coagulate
within a vacant arbour patrolled
by violins and whirlwinds.

Citizens,
this is Cyprus,
this is the Law.

Bye bye children, bye bye.

A Head

Orpheus is scattered, where shall we look for him?
in this draggle-brained compendium, full of bodged
speculations and unseemly characters, including as a matter of fact
the dupe himself, as character a speculation
barely half-decent.

Shall we set out in our boat
gliding between flukes and islands on premonitory breezes,
tracking a dare we initially ran away from
running and running? Do we have the energy for that
at our age, or the guts? Will we mind if it bites us?

Or doesn't? Or mind if it offers us a rare gift
too late to be useful or exciting? We have lost interest in treasure,
(not) but our boat is frail, fashioned of chasms like everything else,
unreliable distinctions etcetera. How could we expect to get home
with that lump in the gunnels?

And why would we want to be wanting to go home anyway,
and where? And where shall we look for Orpheus?
Big fish-head stuck in a crack
or bobbing out happy to have someone to talk to probably.

Araby

Even the hooligans are appalled
by the Moor's behaviour;

each time he appears
his attitude just gets worse,

unjustifiable except
in the light of its own logic:

soap-opera eschatology
and rhythm, snappety-tap.

Just clearing the paths, ok?
But who's egging him on,

if anyone? Where's Vlad
when all this is happening?

Where's Emily come to that?
Watching snails flow

under a privet hedge.
It may even be a case

of mistaken identity:
an assumption's made

then everyone venerates the assumption.
He looks freer somehow,

leaner, less liable to distortion;
has ditched his buttock,

his timbre his tunic his nine moons.
Just clearing the paths

for the story: in araby
he loved a genie,

once upon a time
a genie in old araby.

Door

OK: the miracle (that was the last gift
he paid for), a miracle he did not believe in,
ever, would never happen, never never;
the door had shut on the room that was always
shut; the glimpse that was always wakening
speech in his thumbs. Stars tumble now through a web
of veins, but it's just a night, just a silt
settling in a pond, the offerings, all the golden
paraphernalia of deleted longing -
tripods, a buckle. A door shut
on nothing that could ever have been his, on a face
that was a stone in a stone carapace,
there and forever there where the wood ends,
there and forever.

Tideline

Orpheus just goes straight
on wham through the jaws,
not stopping for anything.

Gulp. Our colomber
didn't mean to be a portal
into a disaster area.

Already forgotten now,
just a few scraps
spattered along the tideline

with bits of net,
shampoo bottles, oil drums,
and driftwood.

Arbour

The arbour is cree:
no matter how many crimes you've committed
or were running towards,
the arbour is repose,

intelligibility, reward,
is its own task and glamour;
a mottled shadow in the core
awaits a firstcomer,

whom nobody after that may approach
or question. It's all in the pose:
a climbing rose on its arch
flaunts a line of beauty,

doves skimming down the gyres,
as light gathers flashing
from all the coigns of the body,
mingling its flame

with that fine composite flame
emitted by the many
who haunt the avenues running,
or sway in the appletrees;

where Sylvio's faun treads,
picking its way, dripping its drops
from which warriors spring:
killers, impalers, revolutionaries,

assembling heaven there
in a bed of lilies.
The arbour is pure loss,
the arbour is mourning.

Notes.

Page 20: Sooty and Sweep were popular glove-puppet TV characters, originally created by Harry Corbett.

Page 28: "Younghusband's wood" refers to what was once a local landmark in the Fairwater area of Cardiff. Similarly "the biscuit factory" (Jacobs).

Page 30: Rollscourt Avenue is a street in Herne Hill, South London.

Page 31: Mangeclous is the eponymous hero of the 1938 book of that name, by the French writer, Albert Cohen. Vronsky refers to a character in Tolstoy's *Anna Karenina* (1873).

Page 43: Orlando Gibbons (1583 - 1625) was one of the leading English composers of his time.

Page 54: "Sylvio" refers to a figure in Andrew Marvell's poem: *The Nymph Complaining for the Death of her Fawn.*

ESTUARINE
(A Death in the Family)

In St Andrews church in Awre there is an ancient and very splendid wooden chest. Its original purpose may have been to hold documents and vestments, but in addition it is believed that corpses recovered from the Severn were placed in it until their burial.
(Abandoned Communities Website)

...the cadaver is not in its place. Where is it?
(Maurice Blanchot, *The Space of the Imaginary*)

Mourning

Her scream cleaves
what it sees

           honour it

honour it she asks
reparation but not her
but me asking it for her

                scream

could I hold it
back the whole lot all of it
spittled out on the table

Beached

Out there in a middle-space
in a blind crook
of urges
      that grey-slathering
heave that declining
squander beached all ends up
in a sticking-place
             flensed
of his luck was it his
or mine his I can't
remember now or believe
in that membrane
          magnanimous
form do you know your name
is it different
spoken there
      are you different

Salt

By gorge by delta
silts
love engrossed

grasses trembling at the edge
you think
almost picturesque

hard to build here before
salt's leached
            the very 'thief
of time'

works the ham
in the air sweating
its grume out

Spars

Difficult to imagine
how when a gull dipped
a ripple winked on a sandbank
(wreck) there was still
even yes even still
still further to reach out
still some clear slope with its jetty
(ordinary tidal river
neither myth nor providence)
how if he'd disembarked
there anywhere I'd be there
to greet him that would be
a shock but a pleasant one
he'd say here look take it
it's yours take it I'd take it
impossible to understand
what I might have been doing there
or whether I came back

Erosion

She is learning to drown
in air her profound study
dissolution of colloids
gradual then all of a sudden
to the big push
tackle rosebush lath
some outpost put to the sword
streaming off into archive
item he is teaching her
to go with the dwellings
into the qualmless drift

The Box at Awre

What I know now about the spars
in the sand his knees
under that sheet (wreck)
just think of it the cries
muffled but getting through
to the daydream with its
appurtenances corbels
plate in a wooden box
with three locks it took
three men papers too
no room for a corpse in there
his knees a tall man broken

Watch

Tormented narrows
He in his authenticity
She in her authenticity

to give to swallow
at the necessary point
all the forces ready for it

glottally inhibited
her egg abandoned
in the next room

It Builds

It builds there it's not
the place to build
                              maybe
it will be cribs brunt
the sediments shush away
stand their ground
I've researched
the whole thing although not
in very much depth as usual
curse of the dilettantes
when concentration
slips to be overborne
by eternity
word in the bible

Nutritional

So many chews
to the spoonful
                  detritus
pouched
swallowing
is another matter though

to be referred

and even when the last banks crumble
scattering equipment
she works a meaning

through flesh and fruit
in the purity of a closed chamber
hallowed by liquors

Waste

On top of everything tritium
isotope of hydrogen
70 nanoGrays per hour
flushed down off the hills
memories memories
everything goes in
and stays in
no need to reject anything
welcome welcome welcome

Flow

His openness though
is obscene
                    the slurry
runs through with a lurch
and back again with a shattering
unholy gargle

she holds what she has
how it is and where it is

demure

Notion of a Weir

Kept trying to adjust things
weir disturbs matters
channels clam up
a "number of spirited gentlemen"
keep digging them out
but we lose heart
and capital one current
elbows another current
elbows the goosander
just shift your ports mate

Smile

His face swarming up
through braids shoals through microbial
scarves out of shadow
tensing flares suddenly
into light breaking through
in the middle-place mint
from the clearing his smile shaping
and focusing rapt battening
down clean over the burred edges
to soften to sink back
again into that tide's
sprawled ceremonies forgetting
it was given and meant
something all the rest
falls away a treasure once
breach
where the alias gets in.

Address to the Box at Awre

box are you listening
even the stone flows
to your law
to the silence
under the dressed arch on the solemn ground

The Bell at Awre

Goes under but not yet quite
we've postponed the moment
mouth you resemble
endlessly your keynote
whistle reeks of disturbed sludge
by the bank under
sewer outlet fosse
where the songs sink back
on themselves autumn leaves ramona
vagina immaculata
witless and folded in
honour it tower
tenor bell in G
(10 cwt 0 qtr 21 lbs)

Equinox

Nibbled constantly
by knives by plaques driving up
and driving back driven
by high winds anyway
just normal stuff going on
three messuages lost
from the parish
                           we await
it trembling the spring wave

ODDMENTS

Brechfa Pool - Elements of the Walk
For Christopher Twigg

1
Each tree its toy island
on the pale water
poised inexplicably,
each gust with a jewel in it:
cache of a grandee.

2
Meadow, slashed
feather-pillow, a fox
drapes the gate dangling
red stole, it conceals
very little except damage.

3
"Barbaric" he calls it
barbaric, muscling
that fleet horse his thighs
barbaric, his tensed squint
barbaric.

4
Toad missed,
overspilling the fête-champêtre:
caviar and wax-bread
fallen out of sync
on the ground, leavings.

5
They came, then. So they came
and they'll come again,
blundering up the banks,
deranged, pornographic.
Spawn rut ponds clumped spunk glut ponds.

6
Lichen-rock, lichen-rock -
plaque summing-up
in remote colours: exequies
for the alien,
the star-lost.

7
On one side a river,
on the other clouds split
the range into discrete humps,
each hill with a relic
in its belly, a creed sleeping.

8
Too cold to stay,
wind blights, currencies
degrade. We are here
but going
home, going.

9
Christopher, your paintings
covered the floor and the mantelpiece.
Apparently a walk
has no edges and may
go on proliferating.

Conversation

(Piero della Francesca)

Back there in the loggia,
something, a bad thing
is happening: whips splay
at their apogee,
homing in.

Outside on the piazza
two men and a youth
are talking; they are looking
in entirely the wrong direction.
Or possibly the men
are discussing that youth,

who may not be real
like them, although solid enough
like them.
It's a sunny day, but the loggia
has its own light-source.

Sealion
(Anselm Kiefer)

Sometimes you can't even get in the bath,
it's so full of little warships, enacting
(that's right - I said enacting, not re-enacting)
some pivotal clash, some ur-splash in the cha-cha-channel.
Admiral Nightmare get out of that tub!

weigh anchor, pull up your hawsers and be gone
and stay gone! Vacate, evacuate if you please
the scene,
for the good of the coming generation.
Some of us are dirty and some of us are cold
and dirty,

what with those little tanks chucking up mud
on the heath. You can't take an innocent stroll
at evening without getting your toes crimped
by some élite (but obsolete) Nibelungian battalion.
More hot-water please,
more soap please,
more bubbles.

The Death of Roy Orbison

Night is a cry,
the night is a drawn-out wail;
a whistle. It fades
and comes back and fades

and has to be searched for,
patiently, with skill,
with the tips of your fingers,
when a path frays
and a breath unravels
in a phosphor crackle.

Night is a pulse,
the night is a gathering wave,
a wake;
is a scent you follow, your eyes shut
from the hut to the boat to the sea.

Carmen

There on the path,
fruit-body five
or six centimetres across,
outer-wall split
into pointed rays, I think five or six
pointed rays, covered
in a thick pinkish-
brown layer, cracked
where the rays bent back
on themselves, leaving it proud
in its saucer:
eyeball,
eyeball, *"Pourquoi...?"* Pale
grey-brown, paler
ring round the slightly-
raised opening. (Spores
dark-brown, globose, warted).
In twig and leaf-mash,
deciduous woodland,
late-summer to autumn.
Eyeball, *"sur mon
chemin."* And the leaves
coming down one by one,
the chestnuts
coming down one
by one.

Earthstar.
Earth.
Star.

The Wood and the Cave
A Chant for Samhain

earth raves in its skin
potentialities imploding
in every available direction

at home in the wrecking-hour
a trashed house in a shivered
grove a man saying

voice man of air
speaking of nothing
the taken the given

tested ground to a paste
with spent roots with the broken
and collapsed bracken

a man of leaves
asking you to take a message
into the hill's corridors

into the grooved hollows
the carious chambers
the flumes the sockets

already too late to be here
already too disenchanted
already too undone to be here

a fate a clearing a charm
a pharmacy a wish
ground in a mortar

carry it to that cave
to that cleft chiseled out by spurts
and drools

to its own echo
its human reverberation
profanity of release and containment

in the dark where the names are
there are no words
in the dark nothing yet

until a voice speaks
in the dark many things
in a wood then the names come

crowd to a lantern-ray
already too lost to be here
already too far gone to be here

a man of fall
of ravagement a plucked fungus
squalid gravid hallucinogenic

speaking of many things
dreaming of many things
dying of many things

a nostrum carry it
you journeying between two folds
lucky

to take the message
to carry it in your own lung
into that hill

where the names wait for you
where the names wait for the lantern
of your voice only

dance in their gibberish
in their blind scrawl
in their diffuse frenzy

already too alive to be here
too amorous too emphatic
already too definitive to be here

making a hill speak
a city under a hill
dance on a fire-spout

with the year's dying shout
caverns blundering into caverns
names into names

a man in a wood speaking to you now
giving you this message now
a breath only

Lyndon Davies was born in Cardiff and now lives in Powys. His critical essays and reviews have appeared regularly in Poetry Wales and his poetry has appeared in many magazines as well as in the anthologies *The Pterodactyl's Wing* (Parthian) and *POETRY WALES Forty Years* (Seren). He edits an irregular internet magazine called Junction Box which features prose-writing by poets and artists. He is a co-organiser with Graham Hartill and Penny Hallas of the Glasfryn Seminars, a series of discussion groups and events centered around literature and art. He was also co-organiser, with John Goodby, of the Poetry Jamboree, a festival of innovative poetries.

AQUIFER